How to love a
TEXAN

Written By:
H. (Skeeter) Kavet

Illustrated By:
Martin Riskin

Manufactured in the United States of America

30 29 28 27 26 25 24 23 22 21 20 19 18 17 16 15 14 13 12 11 10 9 8 7 6 5 4 3 2 1

Ivory Tower Publishing Co., Inc.
125 Walnut St., P.O. Box 9132, Watertown, MA 02272-9132
Telephone #: (617) 923-1111   Fax #: (617) 923-8839

You love a TEXAN by...

Burning out their taste buds with jalapeño peppers.

You love a TEXAN by...

Telling them the latest Aggie jokes.

You love a **TEXAN** by...

Helping them appreciate nature by shooting deer, javelina, game birds, varmints and rabbits.

You love a TEXAN by...

Letting them borrow your pick-up during hunting season.

You love a TEXAN by...

Agreeing with them about how wonderful the weather is.

You love a TEXAN by...

Agreeing with them about how terrible the weather is.

You love a **TEXAN** by...

Watching reruns of "Lonesome Dove" with them each weekend.

You love a TEXAN by...

Explaining to them what a traffic jam is.

You love a **TEXAN** by...

Knowing they caught the animal that makes up their hat bands.

You love a TEXAN by...

Realizing a person's pick-up can be their castle.

You love a TEXAN by...

Pretending to understand their accent.

You love a TEXAN by...

Not getting involved in neighborhood disputes.

You love a TEXAN by...

Supporting their local football team.

You love a TEXAN by...

Agreeing that their chili is just a mite hot.

You love a **TEXAN** by...

Spoiling their pets rotten.

You love a **TEXAN** by...

Celebrating San Jacinto Day with them.

You love a TEXAN by...

Pretending to be impressed with their spread.

You love a TEXAN by...

Making them REAL coffee in the morning.

You love a TEXAN by...

Cooperating during extreme weather conditions.

You love a TEXAN by...

Controlling your comments on their driving.

You love a TEXAN by...

Humoring them when they refer to their 1/2 acre as a ranch.

You love a TEXAN by...

Enduring a tractor pull on a holiday weekend.

You love a **TEXAN** by...

Being patient when they talk slowly.

You love a **TEXAN** by...

Accepting their violence as a satisfactory solution to certain problems.

You love a **TEXAN** by...

Marveling at their knowledge of the back country.

You love a **TEXAN** by...

Dining with them at a favorite restaurant.

You love a TEXAN by...

Vacationing in Colorado to cool off in the summer.

You love a TEXAN by...

Expecting a gun or a dog for your birthday present.

You love a TEXAN by...

Realizing some parts of a man's home really are his castle.

You love a TEXAN by...

Visualizing that warm Texas heart under the gruff exterior.

You love a **TEXAN** by...

Allowing a few friends to bunk out with you.

You love a TEXAN by...

Calling them 'Skeeter' or 'Red' or 'Bones,' instead of their given name which might be something like Horace or Melvin.

You love a **TEXAN** by...

Enjoying the romance of the wide open spaces.

You love a **TEXAN** by...

Getting them real good seats at a rodeo.

You love a **TEXAN** by...

Sharing a parking space in Dallas.

You love a **TEXAN** by...

Asking them to join a panel of experts.

You love a TEXAN by...

Being sure to take off your spurs before going to bed.

You love a **TEXAN** by...

**Rushing to their defense when their belt buckle
sets off a security alarm.**

You love a **TEXAN** by...

Going cow tipping after you've had a few.

You love a TEXAN by...

Knowing that "almost" DOES count when you're pitching horseshoes.

You love a **TEXAN** by...

Showing proper respect for "the ladies."

You love a TEXAN by...

Supporting their duly elected officials.

You love a TEXAN by...

Never hogging their favorite chair.

You love a TEXAN by...

Remembering their birthday with something special.

You love a **TEXAN** by...

Learning the latest Texas dance step.

You love a TEXAN by...

Bringing them nothing smaller than a .38 for personal protection.

You love a TEXAN by...

Idolizing the Rangers except when they are after you.

You love a TEXAN by...

Sharing the road with some of the indigenous wildlife.

You love a TEXAN by...

Convincing them that grits ARE a part of a good Texas breakfast.

You love a TEXAN by...

Supporting your town's football coach.

You love a **TEXAN** by...

Encouraging traditional family values.

You love a TEXAN by...

Remembering how they take their coffee.

You love a TEXAN by...

Sharing your air conditioner on a hot day.

You love a TEXAN by...

Helping them enjoy their Yankee friends.

You love a TEXAN by...

Forgiving a neighbor when their animals get out of hand.

You love a **TEXAN** by...

Recognizing an old buddy you haven't see in years.

You love a **TEXAN** by...

Having a barbecue when relatives come to town.

You love a TEXAN by...

Carrying out a random act of kindness.

You love a **TEXAN** by...

Trying to believe their level of sophistication has improved in recent years.

You love a TEXAN by...

Appreciating the cultural diversity of the state.

You love a **TEXAN** by...

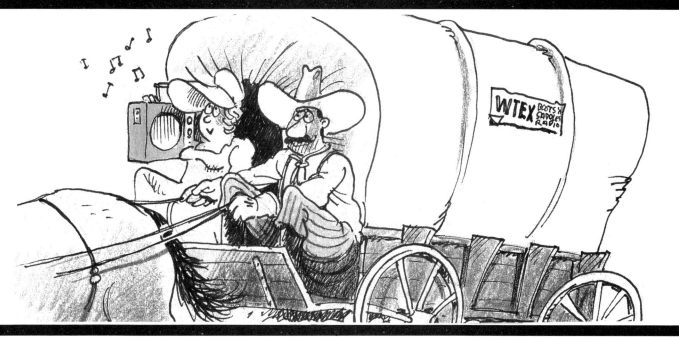

**Devoting at least one button on your radio to
a country music station.**

You love a TEXAN by...

Allowing friends' livestock to water at your tank.

You love a **TEXAN** by...

Dressing so you'll fit in with the crowd.

You love a TEXAN by...

Rescuing folks who believed the weather predictions.

You love a TEXAN by...

Serving salsa and tortilla chips while company is waiting for dinner.

You love a **TEXAN** by...

Never complaining about the conditions of their pick-up.

You love a TEXAN by...

Helping your kicker find his way home after a night at the honkey-tonk.

You love a TEXAN by...

Viewing the West-Texas Stars together.

You love a **TEXAN** by...

Being tolerant of their hunting dogs.

You love a TEXAN by...

Serving some iced tea the moment they get home.

You love a TEXAN by...

Giving them some antacid pills after a meal of chicken-fried steak.

You love a TEXAN by...

Sharing the location of your favorite smokehouse.

You love a **TEXAN** by...

Never insulting their taste buds by putting beans in their chili.

You love a TEXAN by...

**Encouraging them to ignore the temptations
of all the beautiful women.**

You love a TEXAN by...

Bringing the extra tube of longnecks on a river trip.

You love a **TEXAN** by...

Helping to keep their yard bug-free.

You love a TEXAN by...

Appreciating how hard some folks work for their money.

You love a TEXAN by...

Acting blasé when you see someone famous.

You love a TEXAN by...

Keeping fit together.

You love a TEXAN by...

Sharing a shelter during a storm.

You love a TEXAN by...

Teaching them the Texas 2-step or Cotton Eyed Joe.

You love a TEXAN by...

Letting friends know you have biting ants in your yard.

You love a TEXAN by...

Giving an occasional right of way to an armadillo.

You love a **TEXAN** by...

Helping them out in a dry town.

You love a TEXAN by...

Believing all their stories about their ranch and their oil wells.

Other books we publish are available at many fine stores. If you can't find them, send directly to us. $7.00 postpaid

2400-How To Have Sex On Your Birthday. Finding a partner, special birthday sex positions and much more.

2402-Confessions From The Bathroom. There are things in this book that happen to all of us that none of us ever talk about, like the Gas Station Dump, the Corn Niblet Dump and more.

2403-The Good Bonking Guide. A great new term for doing "you know what". Bonking in the dark, bonking all night long, improving your bonking, and everything else you ever wanted to know.

2407-40 Happens. When being out of prune juice ruins your whole day and you realize anyone with the energy to do it on a weeknight must be a sex maniac.

2408-30 Happens. When you take out a lifetime membership at your health club, and you still wonder when the baby fat will finally disappear.

2409-50 Happens. When you remember when "made in Japan" meant something that didn't work, and you can't remember what you went to the top of the stairs for.

2411-The Geriatric Sex Guide. It's not his mind that needs expanding; and you're in the mood now, but by the time you're naked, you won't be!

2412-Golf Shots. What excuses to use to play through first, ways to distract your opponent, and when and where a true golfer is willing to play.

2414-60 Happens. When your kids start to look middle-aged, when software is some kind of comfortable underwear, and when your hearing is perfect if everyone would just stop mumbling.

2416-The Absolutely Worst Fart Book. The First Date Fart, The Lovers' Fart, The Doctor's Exam Room Fart and more.

2417-Women Over 30 Are Better Be- cause... Their nightmares about exams are starting to fade and their handbags can sustain life for about a week with no outside support whatsoever.

2418-9 Months In The Sac. Pregnancy through the eyes of the baby, such as: why do pregnant women have to go to the bathroom as soon as they get to the store, and why does baby start doing aerobics when it's time to sleep?

2419-Cucumbers Are Better Than Men Because... Cucumbers are always ready when you are and cucumbers will never hear "yes, yes" when you're saying "NO, NO."

2421-Honeymoon Guide. From The Advantages Of Undressing With The Light On (it's easier to undo a bra) to What Men Want Most (being allowed to sleep right afterwards without having to talk about love).

2422-Eat Yourself Healthy. Calories only add up if the food is consumed at a table—snacking doesn't count. Green M&M's are full of the same vitamins found in broccoli and more useful eating information your mother never told you.

2423-Is There Sex After 40? She liked you better when the bulge above your waist used to be the bulge in your trousers. He thinks wife-swapping means getting someone else to cook for you.

2424-Is There Sex After 50? Going to bed early just means a chance to catch up on your reading or watch a little extra TV, and you actually miss trying to make love quietly so as not to wake the kids.

2425-Women Over 40 Are Better Because... They realize that no matter how many sit-ups and leg raises they do, they cannot recapture their 17-year-old figures—but they can find something

attractive in any 21-year-old guy.

2426-Women Over 50 Are Better Because... More reasons why women over 50 are better: They will be amused if you take them parking, and they know that being alone is better than being with someone they don't like.

2427-You Know You're Over The Hill When... All the stories of your youth have bored most acquaintances several times over. You're resigned to being slightly overweight after trying every diet that has come along in the last 15 years.

2428-Beer Is Better Than Women Because (Part II)... A beer doesn't get upset if you call it by the wrong name; and after several beers, you can roll over and go to sleep without having to talk about love.

2429-Married To A Computer. You fondle it daily, you keep in touch when you're travelling and you stare at it a lot without understanding it.

2430-Is There Sex After 30? Parking isn't as much fun as it was in high school. He thinks foreplay means parading around nude in front of the mirror, holding his stomach in; and she has found that the quickest way to get rid of an unwanted date is to start talking about commitment.

2431-Happy Birthday You Old Fart! You spend less and less time between visits to a toilet, your back goes out more than you do and you leave programming the VCR to people under 25.

2432-Big Weenies. Why some people have big weenies while other people have teenie weenies; as well as the kinds of men who possess a member, a rod and a wang—and more!

2433-Games You Can Play With Your

Pussy. Why everyone should have a pussy; how to give a pussy a bath (grease the sides of the tub so it can't claw its way out); and more!

2434-Sex And Marriage. What wives want out of marriage (romance, respect and a Bloomingdale's Charge Card); what husbands want out of marriage (to be allowed to go to sleep after sex).

2435-Diapers, Doo-Doo & Diddlypoop Baby's First Year. How much will it cost, the secrets of midnight feedings, do diapers really cause leprosy and other vital info for parents.

2436-How To Love A New Yorker. You love a New Yorker by pretending to understand their accent, sharing a parking space, getting it for them wholesale and realizing they look at "Out of Towners" as a supplemental source of income.

2437-The Retirement Book. Brings the retiree up to date on Early Bird Specials, finding their bifocals, dressing like a retired person and remembering important things like paying for the book.

2438-Dog Farts. They do it under the table, in front of the TV, on the way to the vet and after devouring some horrible animal they caught in the yard. This book describes them all.

2439-Handling His Midlife Crisis. By treating him like a child when he wants to feel young again, consoling him when he goes from bikinis to boxer shorts and making sure he has something green with each meal besides Heineken beer.

2440-How To Love A Texan. You love a Texan by agreeing that their chili is just a mite hot, humoring them when they refer to their half acre as a ranch and rushing to help when their belt buckle sets off a security alarm.

Ivory Tower Publishing Co., Inc., 125 Walnut St., P.O. Box 9132, Watertown, MA 02272-9132   Tel: (617) 923-1111